A Divorce Recovery Interactive Devotional

Vernique Esther

Copyright © 2020 When Seasons Change.

No part of this publication may be reproduced, distributed, or transmitted in any form or by any means, including photocopying, recording, or other electronic or mechanical methods, without the prior written permission of the authors.

Unless otherwise expressed, all quotations and references must be permitted by the Author. All Scripture references from NKJ and NIV Bibles. Cover Design: Designed by Maejor.
For information regarding special discounts for bulk purchases of this book, for charitable donation, or for speaking engagements, please visit: www.authenticallywed.com
or email admin@authenticallywed.com

ISBN: 978-0-578-65223-8 imprint - Vernique Esther, LMSW, United States

Published by JWG Publishing @www.businessstartupacademy.live/bookpublishing
Printed in the United States of America.

When Seasons Change

Acknowledgements

I really wish I had the time and page space to thank every single person who helped me on this journey. Not just the people who helped to complete this book, but those who helped me on my personal journey towards healing and wholeness. They are personal heroes to me.

I would first like to thank my mother, Paulette Barthelus. Thank you for making me the resilient and headstrong woman I am. The best parts of you have somehow become my inheritance, and I'm grateful. Then my Godmother, Myrtha Hyppolite who, years ago, told me she had visions of me writing books. You have been my biggest cheerleader, encourager, and confidante; thank you for believing in me.

To my accountability partners in life and business: Brittney Holmes Jackson, Alexandria Mann, Brittany Broaddus-Smith, and Zaykeria Miranda, thank you.

To the women who walked with me through the darkest season of my life: Faith-Tomi Wilson, Leah Hayes, Isa Tatum, Talia Sylvain, Nickeya Brown, Nikita Freeman, Lydia Smith, Anna Oakley, and Calandra Togba-Doya. I love each of you and you will never know how much your words, love, space, and time impacted me.

To my grandmother, Pauvrera, who is the only human being I live to make proud. I hope my life honors you in a way that reminds you of the redemptive nature of God.

Lastly, yet most importantly, to an all-righteous, all-sovereign, all-good God. This wasn't a fire You intended for me to walk through, but You made sure, on the other side, that I *became* the fire. I will forever give my life to serve the One who gave it all for me. It is for Your glory that this exists.

Contents

Introduction – Anchored in Christ 9

Season 1 – Acknowledge the Offense 17

Season 2 – Deciphering the Truth From the Lies 33

Season 3 – Grief 49

Season 4 – Forgiveness 63

Season 5 – Self-Care 77

Season 6 – My New Normal 89

Author page 103

Note from the Author

The *why* behind this book is relatively obvious. I have personally experienced divorce. It was truly the hardest and most distressing season of my entire life. However, I survived, and I promised that if God could pull me out of the hell of divorce, I would be faithful to go back into the trenches and pull others out. So, here I am in the trenches with you, beloved, and you're so worth it. I honestly had zero plans to write a book. As a matter of fact, I planned to be divorced, work a job, and live as quietly as possible because I felt I had committed an inexcusable social failure.

Then God laughed. So, here I am being an entrepreneur, leading a community of people in the realm of authentic and healthy relationships, and talking to you. It's absolutely insane, but I love every part of it. I'm living a life I never dreamed of and it's all because I chose to heal.

You have to CHOOSE to heal. It's an intentional, day-in and day-out process. It's messy and there's no official rulebook to it, but you know when you're on the right path.

I can tell you from experience, real life transformation is possible. People often allow divorce to destroy any and every chance of them living again. They grow bitter, angry, and there's a deadness in their approach to life. This does not have to be you, and recovery does not have to take years.

Divorce provoked something in me that I didn't know was there. If you find yourself facing a divorce, let this trial refine you in such a way that what comes out of you is the purest of gold. God wants to make you whole again so you can experience the abundant life He promised you. And you, my dear friend, have decided to spend part of your season with me. I am honored. Let's get started.

This devotional has a method! In it you will find:

6 Seasons – This is where I simply expound on the dedicated topic of the season that I believe will help you recover healthily at any stage in your divorce journey.

Season Assignment – Every season in life comes with an assignment, or focus. In this book, you will have an assignment that is thought-provoking and challenging. This is where you will put the concepts into action.

Deep Dive – Along with the assignments, you will have questions that allow you to fully think through and process the season and help you introspectively dive deeper.

Pause Point – In each season, I have given you free access to video content where I expound *even further* on the topic and speak directly to your heart.

Emotional Checkpoint – How do you feel today? Which emotions have you felt most lately? You will be asked to identify your emotions in the chart and briefly write out your thoughts.

Devotional – We end the season with scriptural application and a prayer to seal the work that has been done!

Thought Space – We could not forget to include free writing space for any additional thoughts, revelations from the season or prayers.

Introduction

Anchored in Christ

Dearly Beloved,

We are gathered here today because, whether expectedly or unexpectedly, we have unfortunately become acquainted with the life-sucking, soul-crushing, peace-stealing experience that is divorce. It is a fate we would not dare call upon our worst enemy and yet...it is ours to endure. It's not fair. It isn't right. Life was NOT supposed to go like this. You may be angry. You may be anguished. You may even feel regretful, lost, depressed, anxious, and/or broken into a million pieces. All of it is warranted. However, what you cannot do during this time is turn away from the Lover of your soul.

Here's a secret I'm going to give to you early on in this journey: the hardest way to do this is **without** God. Listen, He may be one of the people you're angry with, but unlike the others in your life, He can handle it. The questions, the emotions, and the pain don't scare Him. He wants it all.

During this process, you're going to feel lost – like you're floating from moment to moment without any control – however, if you make Christ your anchor, He will make sure you're secure, cared for, and never too far from His grace.

No, this was not the life you intended. Yes, your world and life, as you know it, is crumbling, but the truth remains that greater is He that is in you than He that is in the world (1 John 4:4). The enemy indeed came in like a flood, but if you allow God to, He will raise up a standard against him so that you will not be consumed (Isaiah 59:19). I beg of you, do not forsake the place of prayer for a grave of bitterness. If you're going to be broken, do it in the arms of Jesus.

Here's the reality: with Jesus or not, this season will not be without pain or difficulties, BUT if there is anything to find solace in, it's this..."The LORD is close to the brokenhearted; He rescues those whose spirits are crushed" (Psalm 34:18). So, while we are here, let's lay ourselves at His feet.

Lord it's us... the brokenhearted. Would You draw near to us in this moment, even this season? We need You now, more than ever. We are crushed, we are anguished, and we have nowhere else to turn. Our backs are against the biggest wall we've ever seen, and it seems like we will suffocate under the weight of our varying emotions, but we are choosing to do this Your way. You didn't promise it would be easy, but You did promise it would work together for our good. Help us not to lose heart, help us to find peace in the midst of this chaos, and help us to see You in light of Your glory, instead of our tragedy. We are ready and willing to heal, so we can walk in the power and authority that is our portion as Your sons and daughters. We trust You, Father. Turn our bitterness into sweetness. In Jesus' Name.

Your season has just changed or has been changing in huge way, and, just like natural seasons, they will continue to change. I have broken up this interactive devotional into seasons because similar to natural seasons; each comes with their discomforts. What makes them unique is that they are marked by their changes from the season before. The seasons in this book are the spaces you need to traverse in order to get to the place called healing. Each season has its own process, and we will address each one as intentionally as possible to maximize your time here. This is not going to be the devotional where you feel cute and cuddly afterward. You honestly may get upset with me for unearthing things you did not know were there. That is okay.

If we are going to be diligent about healing, we have to do some triage. **I highly recommend taking any thoughts and feelings to a licensed professional counselor.**

You will notice there is no timed expectation of completion for this interactive devotional. My intent is that you go through this at your own pace. You may consume it all in a month, or maybe it will take you 6 months. This is about you journeying through every season the way you need to, however, I do have a warning. When it comes to divorce recovery, people often hold on to the pain much longer than they have to. If it takes you a while to work through this devotional, make sure it is because you need to, and not because you're scared to peel back the layers of your heart.

Pause Point

Pause here and take time to watch a quick introductory video then dive into the rest of the book.
There are three ways to access the videos:

1. Open your phone's camera app and focus on the QR code. Follow the prompted link.
2. Download a QR code reader app from your apps store and use it to read the code.
3. Go to your web browser and type: www.authenticallywed.com/wscpausepoint.

Deep Dive

What 3 things do you hope to get from this workbook, and why are they important to you?

What do you need from God today? Write what's on your heart.

Season 1
Acknowledge the Offense

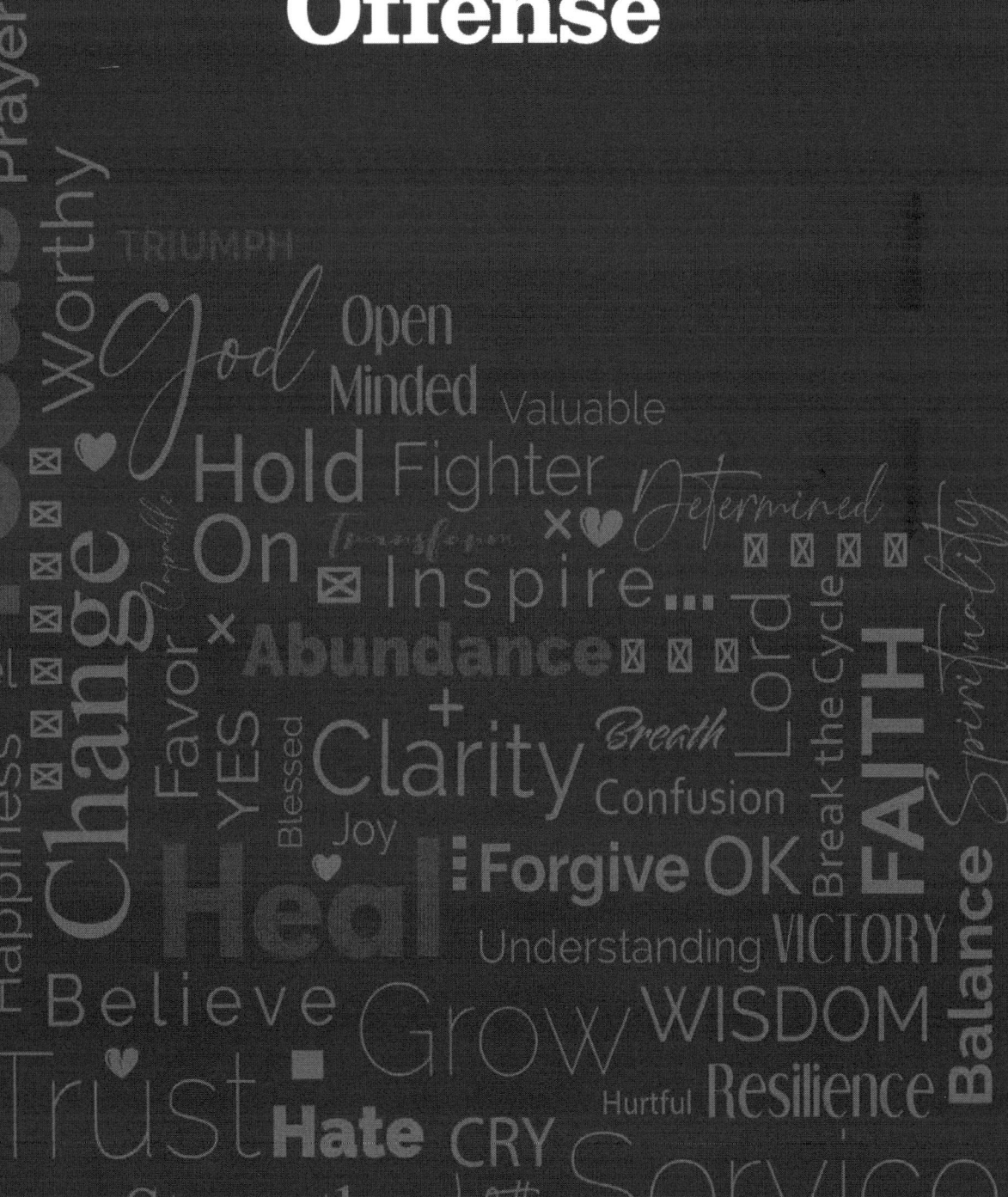

When it comes to healing from broken relationships, people often preach forgiveness, as though it's easy when in actuality you do a disservice to yourself to jump straight to forgiveness without acknowledging what happened. *What do I mean?* Traumatic experiences, like divorce, come at you fast and often feel like a whirlwind of occurrences and emotions. It does not leave much room for processing—taking in what has happened and checking inwardly for how you feel. To swallow whole (forgive) what you are not yet able to digest (process) is cruel. So, let's start the process of unraveling what happened with a few truths:

It happened.

Right now, you are living in the aftermath or in the midst of a traumatic experience. You may not have heard or been told that before, but divorce and broken relationships are traumatic by nature. Trauma is simply a disturbing experience, and divorce in particular, dramatically changes the way we view people, ourselves, relationships, in general, the world, and often God.

It is a trauma no one can see the injuries from, but it is indeed REAL. Further-more, I want you to know that this concept is unbiased. What I mean is, this is traumatic whether you were the offender who ultimately impacted the course of your relationship towards divorce, whether it was mutually toxic, or whether you were completely innocent (and rarely is this true). We are often mistaken in the idea that perhaps an unfaithful or otherwise wrong party has no rights to trauma or hurt. When the truth is, people who violate relationship boundaries are often struggling with their own inner offenses and struggles that led to offending others, especially those in close proximity to them. With that being said, regardless of which side of the "fault fence" you stand on, you have to accept that what occurred in your relationship actually happened.

"It" and you are not okay.

The other truth is, in situations like this, it is easy to want to put on a brave face, smile, and have a predetermined response for when people ask if you're "okay," while you die inside.

Know this: Divorce, and the circumstances that lead to it are not okay, therefore, **you don't have to be.** You've probably heard it a million times before, but I want you to *really* know it: It's okay to not be okay. YOU ARE NOT OKAY!! When you allow yourself to be as not okay as you are, THAT is where God can meet you and begin the process of healing. Prayerfully, and with the help of counseling (preferably), you can be okay again. However, today....it's okay not to be.

Season 1 Assignment

Write down what happened. This may draw tears or anger, but you cannot ignore it and think you will move on. Don't dissect the meaning of the occurrence, simply write it down and at the end write/say, "I acknowledge that all of this happened and it was not okay."

Pause Point

Pause here and take time to watch season 1's video for a more in-depth discussion on acknowledging the offense. Then use the space below to journal your thoughts.

There are three ways to access the videos:

1. Open your phone's camera app and focus on the QR code. Follow the prompted link.
2. Download a QR code reader app from your apps store and use it to read the code.
3. Go to your web browser and type: www.authenticallywed.com/wscpausepoint.

Season 1 Devotional
Psalm 73

As children, we are taught not to question God and to simply "deal" with life as best we can. However, if God never intended for us to question or acknowledge our hurt, then much of Psalms, and even other parts of the Bible, wouldn't make sense.

In Psalm 73, we see Asaph detailing and venting much of his frustrations about the way his life is going, especially concerning his enemies, or those who have wronged him. He goes on for verses about their conduct and how seemingly great their lives are compared to his own.

From our lens, he seems pretty whiny, but if we're honest with ourselves, we have all been there. Sometimes what we have encountered is so emotionally heavy, we need to get raw and honest about how we feel and let it all out before God or **trusted** friends.

Divorce is HARD. There are days where you may experience bitterness, regret, or anger. However, it's imperative that you acknowledge what happened and how it makes you feel because holding it in only creates roots of toxicity and crevasses where the enemy can hide.

The most amazing thing about Psalm 73, however, is that he doesn't just complain then close out the chapter. He acknowledges how he feels, then he acknowledges the Lord. He accepts his current reality, then sets his heart back in position for God to meet him. Facing the facts of where you are does not have to turn into an emotional black hole. You can acknowledge how you feel, give it to God, then set your gaze once again. Acknowledging where you are empties you of the hurt so you have room for healing. It is a needed cleansing.

Father, I thank You that my honesty and experiences don't scare You. I'm grateful that You will hear me vent as much as I need to, during this process and You love me enough to listen. I accept that this is happening/has happened and it hurts. I am still learning how to be honest with myself and where I am, but I ask that You hold my hand through this healing journey. Jesus, I confess that I am not okay and what I experienced/am experiencing is not okay either, as it is neither my or Your will for my life. And I know you will give me grace to overcome.

I thank You that when You died on the cross, You rose with all power and freedom from the effects of trauma. I come against any memory or experience that would attempt to steal my peace. I thank You that as I do the work to be whole, that You would teach me to OWN my experience and use it for Your glory. In Jesus' Name.

Deep Dive

Now that you understand this as a traumatic experience, how does that make you feel? Write your raw, uncut questions and thoughts to God.

"Humility promotes healing."

—Vernique Esther

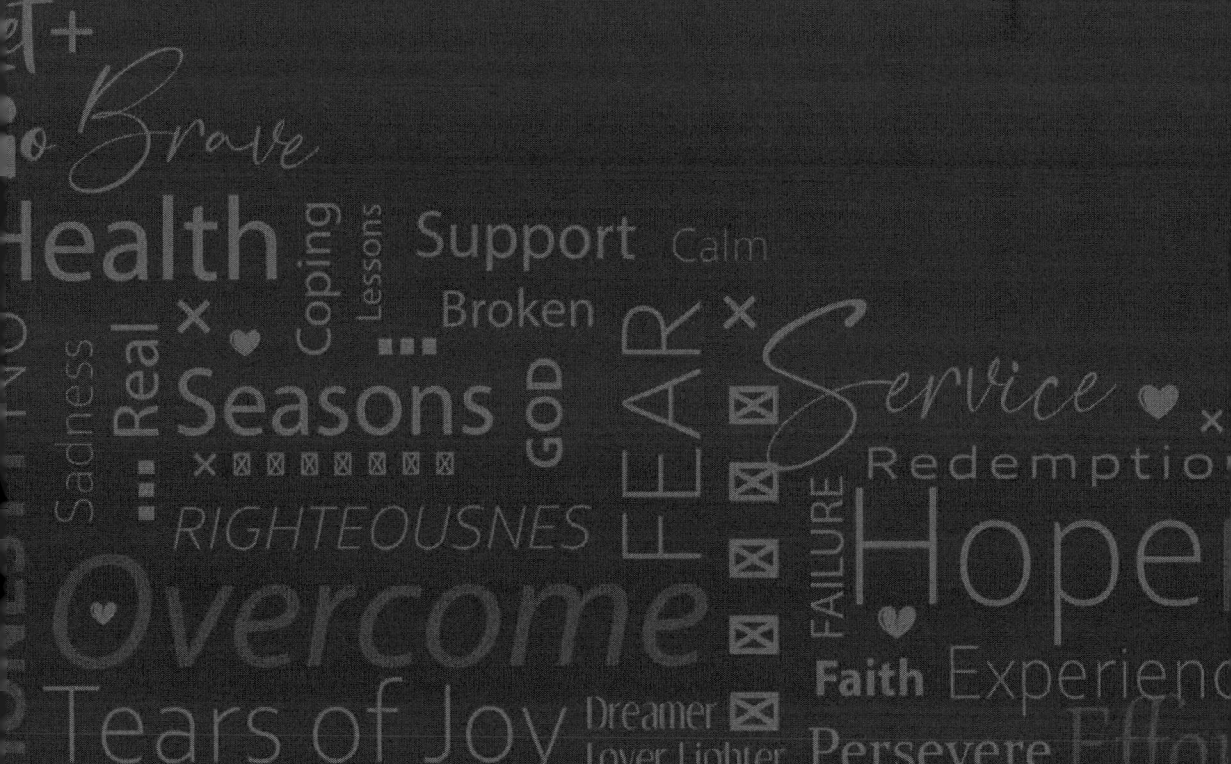

Thought Space

Use this space to journal any additional thoughts or prayers concerning this season.

Emotional Checkpoint

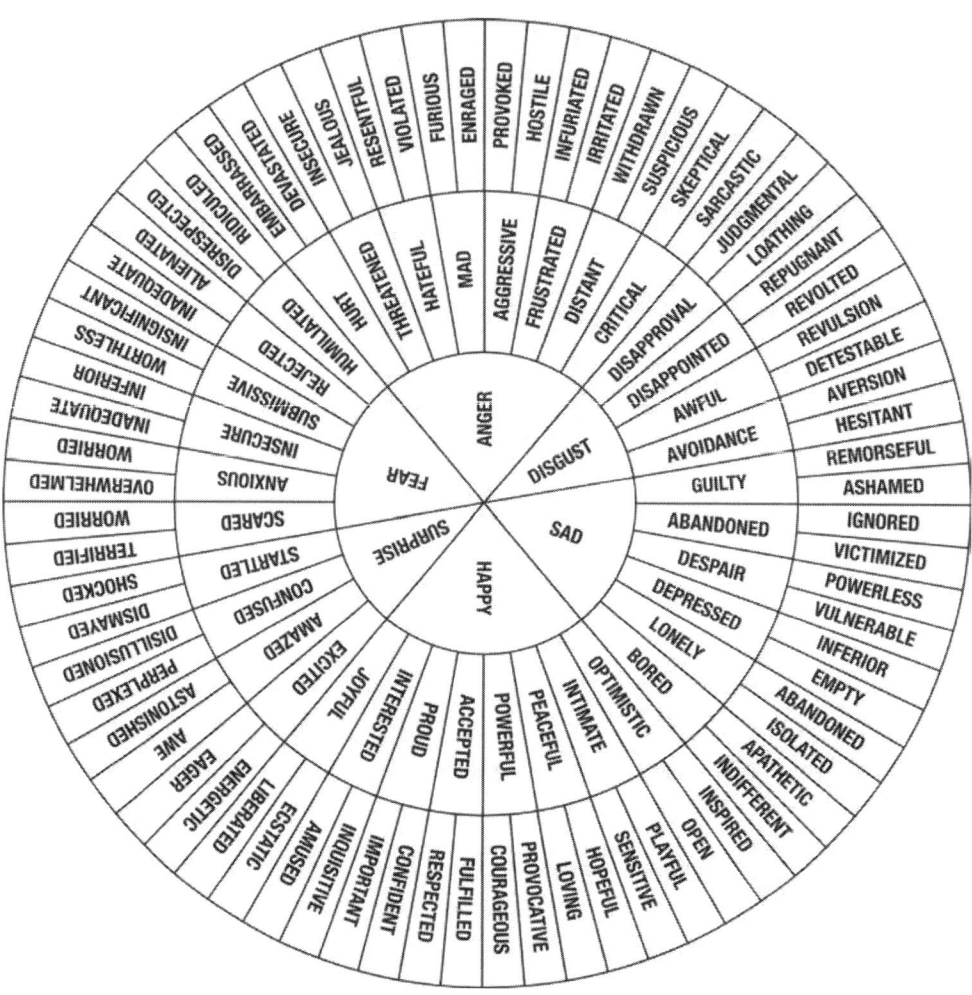

How do you feel today? Which emotions have you felt most lately? Identify your emotions in the chart and briefly write out your thoughts.

_____
_____
_____
_____
_____

Season 2
Deciphering the Truth From the Lies

One of my favorite therapeutic theories is Narrative Therapy. Narrative Therapy looks at the stories people tell themselves and what they mean concerning how people behave or see themselves. I LOVE stories. I will watch documentaries, read articles, and talk to people just to get a good story. Why? Because stories are POWERFUL.

Every day you're alive, you add to the story of yourself, and with each experience, your brain will draw conclusions about what they mean for your relationships and self-perception. As you can imagine, an event as emotionally devastating and life-altering as divorce throws your brain into a frenzy of storytelling.

In the beginning, your emotions may try and tell you that you're not good enough, you'll never be okay, you'll never find love again, and so many other things. Your brain is drawing from the pain you feel, instead of the truth of God, or even reality. The "trick" to overcoming divorce is to feel how you feel, but without ingesting the lies. Every time a lie comes, ask yourself, "Is this true? Would anyone who loves me say this about me?"

The story you tell yourself and the conclusions you draw about who you are, through this process and after, matters. Decide now what you want your story to be, then live from a place that affirms this story. To take it a step further, Narrative Therapy aims to separate *people* from *problems*. The event of divorce does not have to become an internalized marker of who you are.

Your identity and worth are independent of what you have gone through. Consider Joseph. His story can be seen one of two ways: as devastating and full of pain or as a story of endurance and triumph. God wants to give you a beautiful story from the ashes of this season, so you too can say, "what the enemy meant for evil, God used for the saving of many lives" (Genesis 50:20). This is exactly what you will do in your next assignment.

Season 2 Assignment

This season you will break down how you feel and infuse it with God's truth. Whenever you feel intense negative emotions, come back to this assignment and use the following formula to combat them. **"I acknowledge that I feel [insert emotion], however, I refuse to believe [insert lie]. The truth is [insert reality-based statement and/or Scripture]."** Couple this formula with Scripture, prayers and other affirmations. This will assist in the war against the enemy's lies which keep you from receiving God's unfailing love and truth.

When Seasons Change

Pause Point

Pause here and take time to watch season 2's video for a more in-depth discussion on deciphering the truth from the lies. Then use the space below to journal your thoughts.

There are three ways to access the videos:
1. Open your phone's camera app and focus on the QR code. Follow the prompted link.
2. Download a QR code reader app from your apps store and use it to read the code.
3. Go to your web browser and type: www.authenticallywed.com/wscpausepoint.

Season 2 Devotional
2 Corinthians 10:5

Cognitive distortion is a term we use in the counseling arena to describe what happens when our brains convince us something that is untrue is true. The distortion is so good, that people are unable to see beyond them and end up perceiving their lives through this distortion. It often takes the work of a therapist to help unravel the lie and ground a person in truth. Cognitive distortions are internalized statements such as "I never do anything right" or "I'm worthless and unlovable."

Divorce and other traumatic events have this same ability. The enemy often uses our vulnerability during this season to implant lies in our hearts and minds that stand in direct opposition to the heart and truth of God. However, we have the secret weapon for this in 2 Corinthians 10:5. The Word challenges us to take captive every thought that attempts to make Christ a liar.

See, the enemy of our souls is also called the father of lies, and his sole job is to weaken your faith and get you to forfeit the truth of God, so you miss the promises of God. Your job is to declare the Word of God above the loud taunting of the enemy. And, if ever you question whose voice is talking, remember God will never degrade or devalue you. You are precious to Him and He loves you.

Father, I lay my broken heart and fractured mind down at Your feet. I am so consumed by negative thoughts and emotions that I don't know what is true anymore.

Lord, make me into a sheep who knows Your voice (John 10:27), so I won't be drawn away by the voice of the enemy or my own brokenness. Teach me how to take my negative thoughts captive and renew my mind as I do so. Rewrite my story the way You see it, so I'm reminded of my victory in You. I renounce every lie of the enemy and I choose today, and every day, to let You anchor me in Your truth. I refuse to be tossed to and fro by the wavering of my mind (Ephesians 4:14) with each emotion and distortion. I declare, I am steadfast and immovable from this day forward. In Jesus' Name.

Deep Dive

What lies have you or the enemy been whispering? ? What has your mind sounded like lately?

What do you *want* your narrative to be from your experience with divorce? Write your raw, uncut question and thoughts to God.

"Experiencing divorce does not diminish your worth."

—Vernique Esther

Thought Space

Use this space to journal any additional thoughts or prayers concerning this season.

Emotional Checkpoint

How do you feel today? Which emotions have you felt most lately? Identify your emotions in the chart and briefly write out your thoughts.

_____
_____
_____
_____
_____

Season 3

Grief

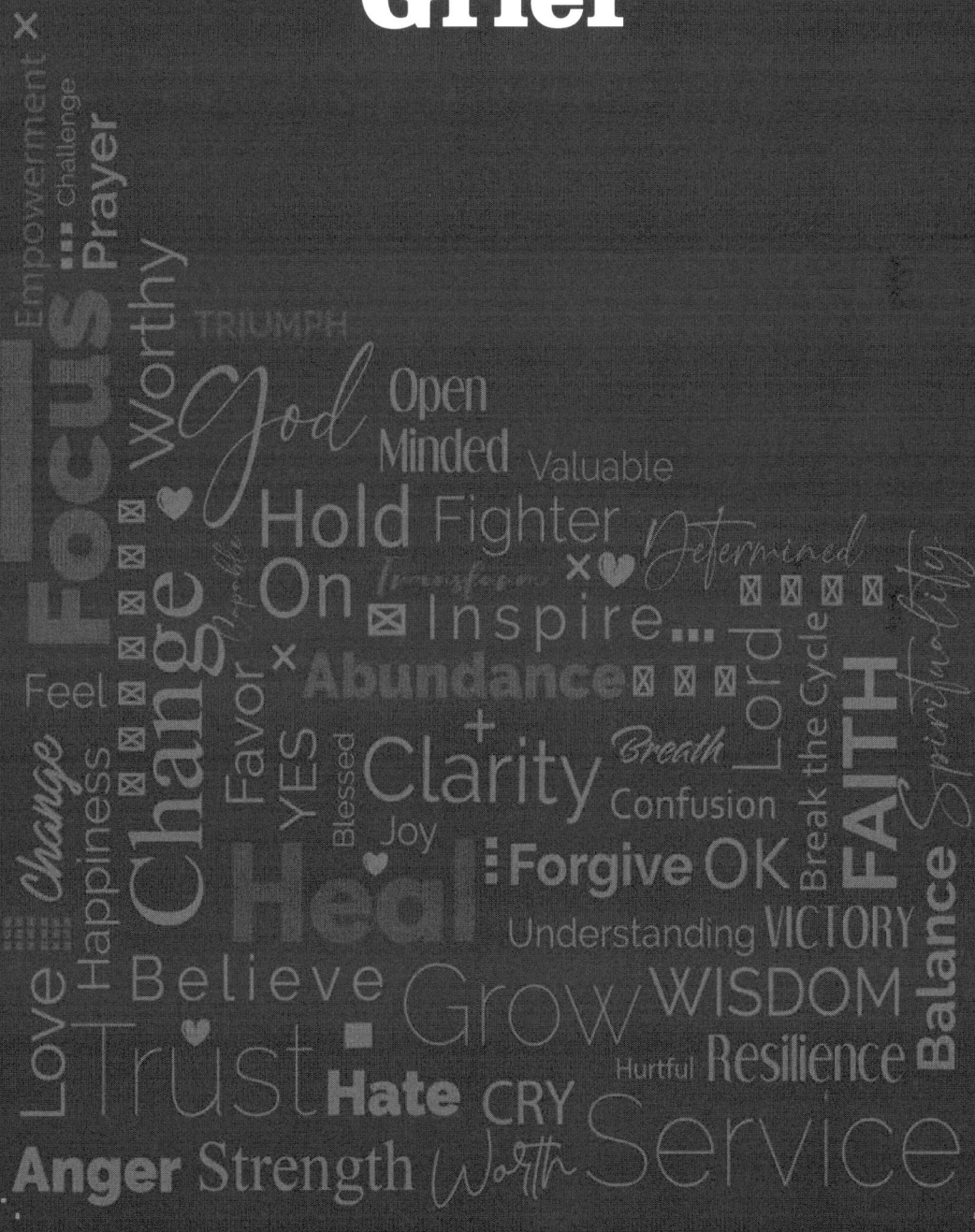

Grief is no longer a term relegated to death alone. It is an experience we will all have throughout our lifetime. My definition of grief is the emotional and mental process by which we mitigate or come to accept loss and failed expectations. With this understanding, we can experience grief due to job termination, status shifts, or relational brokenness like divorce.

As you may have unfortunately figured out, or will, divorce feels like death. You may not have ever died before (hopefully), but when divorce occurs, it could feel like the Grim Reaper is standing at your doorstep beckoning you to come. If you're honest, you would go without a second thought. Let me free you for a moment: if you've ever felt like you'd rather die than live through another day of divorce-filled misery, you are not alone.

The Bible describes marriage as two becoming one flesh (Mark 10:8), which means divorce is the tearing of that flesh. If someone ripped your arm off of your shoulder, it would likely hurt, to say the least. That's essentially divorce. When you stood before God and man, exchanging vows, and pouring out your undying love to one another, you expected to live out your commitment of "til death do us part." However, things didn't go as planned.

Grief is not just a part of divorce; it is a necessary component. It is important to not only grieve, but to grieve well. How do you know you're grieving well? For one, you have to actually let yourself go through it. I get it. You have a job, responsibilities, or maybe you have children, so you can't afford to break down every time you have an intense feeling. However, bottling it all up and throwing on a strong face is not grieving. It's masking. Grief is best done when you give yourself the grace to not be okay, with the understanding that you eventually will be.

You may have heard of the five stages of grief, which we will cover in our upcoming Pause Point. Well, allowing yourself to cycle through each stage – even circling back to certain ones – can be the difference between living wounded or living victoriously.

The reality is you will NEVER be the same again, and you shouldn't want to be. Who you were got you to where you are now; who you need to be will take you into the future. But you won't get to the better part without grieving the bitterness of this season.

Season 3 Assignment

This is going to feel cryptic, but I want you to eulogize your marriage. What would you say if you were standing over the casket of your marriage? What would you want an audience of mourners to know? What lessons are you taking from your experience? Take your time to complete this task.

Pause Point

Pause here and take time to watch season 3's video for a more in-depth discussion on navigating the stages of grief. Then use the space below to journal your thoughts.

There are three ways to access the videos:
1. Open your phone's camera app and focus on the QR code. Follow the prompted link.
2. Download a QR code reader app from your apps store and use it to read the code.
3. Go to your web browser and type: www.authenticallywed.com/wscpausepoint.

Season 3 Devotional
Job 1:1-22

Grieving the loss of someone you love is difficult whether they've actually passed away or the relationship has died. Often, the loss of a relationship hurts more, because there is a certain finality in death that is not afforded when a relationship ends and two living people part ways. The remnants of the relationship, including the person themselves, serve as a taunting reminder of the idealized version of the relationship. It may even evoke feelings of failure and shame.

What do you do when you are dealt the biggest blow of your life? How do you respond when it seems the pain has no end in sight?

Let's consider Job. In the book's first chapter, four messengers come to Job with unfathomable news. They announce that most of his family and material possessions, and everything he had built were gone in an instant. Job had no time to prepare for what was happening or even say goodbye.

You may be feeling like Job in this season. It may seem like life is piling up on you and you're just about to reach your breaking point. However, what we can learn from Job is how to be postured with proper perspective even in the midst of grief. His response in chapter one, and throughout the book, was to still bless the name of the Lord and trust Him. Not once did he "curse God and die," as his wife suggested (Job 2:9). As a matter of fact, one of my favorite verses is when Job says, concerning God, "Though He slay me, yet will I trust in Him" (Job 15:13). In the midst of utter grief and despair, his heart was steadfast in God.

In all honesty, the cure to grief is to go through it, and what preserves you in the midst of mourning is your perspective. It may feel like everything hell has to offer is being thrown at you, but bless God anyway. Let His joy be your strength, even here.

Father, I thank You that I do not serve a High Priest who cannot empathize with my weaknesses (Hebrews 4:15). You are so mindful of where I am, and You're in the midst of my grief. I thank You that in this moment, though I don't have all the words or understanding, I can choose to submit to Your sovereignty and bless Your name. Lord, could You help me to navigate my feelings of sadness and disappointment? I feel lost and unsure. Remind me that You are my rock and my fortress (Psalm 18:2) and I am safe in You.

Help me to manage my, sometimes, explosive emotions because of the depth of pain that I feel. Teach me to be patient with myself as I maneuver through, and grant me the grace to endure. Lord, be a healing balm to my soul. In Jesus' Name.

Deep Dive

What scriptures can you take from the book of Job that will encourage you during this season? What do the scriptures you chose mean to you?

Which stage of grief have you experienced already? What stage(s) are you experiencing now?

> "Grieving is painful, but necessary."

—Vernique Esther

Thought Space

Use this space to journal any additional thoughts or prayers concerning this season.

Emotional Checkpoint

How do you feel today? Which emotions have you felt most lately? Identify your emotions in the chart and briefly write out your thoughts.

_____
_____
_____
_____
_____

Season 4
Forgiveness

Ahhhh, yes...the dreaded word. You've thought it, heard it, got preached to about it, and probably have family and friends telling you how much you need to do it. I don't want to preach to you about why it's important, because you likely already know. I want to talk about what forgiveness is in real life and how to do it.

Forgiveness first starts by looking **inward** at our own condition. Here's the reality: while we were yet sinners, Christ died for us (Romans 5:8). **WHILE** we were sinners, not after. He granted us forgiveness and a way to the Father **in the midst** of our mess, knowing we would hurt and reject Him. So, I have to ask: are we not called to be Christ-like?

If God forgives us repeatedly, if our righteousness is like filthy rags, and if all have sinned and fallen short, why then, when we are wronged, we act as though grace ceases to be sufficient. We so blatantly deem others unworthy of the same forgiveness we have been freely granted daily. Tough stuff, isn't it? The hard and unfortunate truth is that unforgiveness, at its core, is rooted in pride. You read that correctly. Not hurt, not disappointment, not trauma...**pride**.

Here is how I know. If you were riding a bike and suddenly fell off and broke your leg, your first instinct would likely be to focus on the injury and recovery rather than taking offense with the bike. Hurt, disappointment, and trauma yields cries and attempts for treatment and healing, not unforgiveness. When we place ourselves in opposition with Christ's mandate to forgive, we are essentially telling Him, that His death was in vain.

Now, I get it. This is one of the hardest things to do, especially in your situation. However, it becomes easier when we choose to look at a person the way God does. When it comes to your ex-spouse (or anyone else involved), you may not be in the place to accept this change quite yet. God wants healing for them too, and perhaps **your** forgiveness (whether you tell them or not) will draw them towards repentance and wholeness.

The bottom line is this, divorce is grueling enough. Adding unforgiveness and bitterness to the mix only makes it more difficult. What keeps people unhealed from divorce longer than necessary is this **one** piece. You have to release them so you can meet your future sooner rather than later. Here's the secret: It is very hard to withhold forgiveness from someone you pray for.

Pray for them and ask that God show you what He sees when He looks at them. Ask God to remove all bitterness and allow you to see the situation in the spirit (especially in the case of infidelity) and remove broken lenses. Your prayers for them may not be very long or robust and that's okay. Start where you can, however you can.

Season 4 Assignment

Take a moment to write down at least one thing you will commit to pray for your former spouse or any involved parties. It may start with praying that they repent or maybe you could pray that they experience healing for themselves. As you feel led, broaden the list or spend more time in prayer for them.

Pause Point

Pause here and take time to watch season 4's video for a more in-depth discussion on forgiveness. Then use the space below to journal your thoughts.

There are three ways to access the videos:

1. Open your phone's camera app and focus on the QR code. Follow the prompted link.
2. Download a QR code reader app from your apps store and use it to read the code.
3. Go to your web browser and type: www.authenticallywed.com/wscpausepoint.

Season 4 Devotional
Ephesians 4:31-32; Mark 11:25; Hebrews 12:1

I'll admit it, forgiveness comes at a price. It forces us to no longer hold anything over people who may have deeply hurt us. It takes away the power dynamic of being wrong and right, and places you and your offender on a level playing field (in your heart, as forgiveness doesn't retract consequences). It's a tough pill to swallow, however, when we consider that God looks at our willingness to forgive others as His meter for forgiving us, it's a low price to pay (Matthew 6:14). Jesus has set the example by dying for sinners and we are called to the same charge, to kill our flesh and forgive those who trespass against us.

However, usually the "offender" is not the only person needing forgiveness. We often hold grudges against ourselves, especially when experiencing divorce. The blame game and pity parties often reside in the same place and lead us to self-deprecation, self-loathing, and anger.

Here's the good news: You can release yourself from whatever wrong you caused (real or perceived) because Christ has already done so. Ask for forgiveness, then repent. Lay aside whatever sin is holding you back and choose to accept the mercy of God. Jesus knew you would mess up, that's why He gifted us with grace. Hear Him saying this to you, "Go and sin no more" (John 8:11). Remember, the "sin no more" part, but don't forget the command to "go." Move on and go into the future.

Lord, I thank You for modeling forgiveness for me in such a beautiful way. I thank You that You don't see me in light of my latest or biggest mess up, You simply see me, Your beloved. Jesus, would You show me how to forgive like You forgive? Can You give me the right perspective on those who have hurt me? I want to have Your heart towards them, but my pain makes it difficult to see what You see." Restore my vision and remove pride.

Lord, I acknowledge that You have already forgiven me. Help me now to forgive myself. I no longer desire to be bound by my past and desire the freedom You have promised me in Your Word. Help me to see myself, and others, in light of Your wonderful grace. In Jesus' Name.

Deep Dive

What has been the hardest thing to forgive? What makes it hard?

What would it look like for you to forgive? Are there any obstacles keeping you from doing so?

What do you need to forgive yourself for?

> "Don't heal to prove a point. Heal for real."
>
> —Vernique Esther

A Divorce Recovery Interactive Devotional — Vernique Esther, LMSW

Thought Space

Use this space to journal any additional thoughts or prayers concerning this season.

Emotional Checkpoint

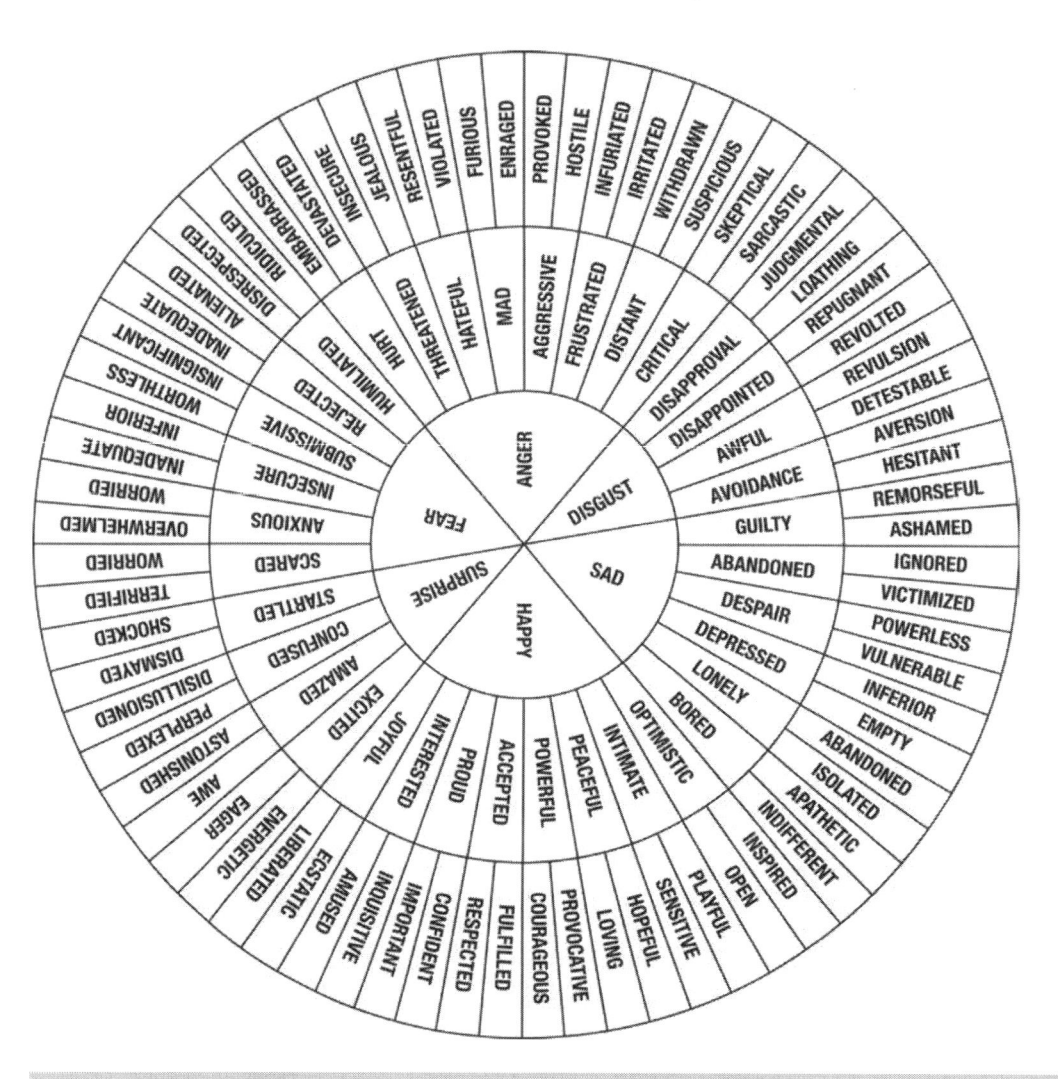

76

How do you feel today? Which emotions have you felt most lately? Identify your emotions in the chart and briefly write out your thoughts.

_____
_____
_____
_____
_____
_____

Season 5

Self-Care

I know, I know! Don't throw this chapter away! Yes, self-care has been the buzzword for the last couple of years, but just because the term is played out doesn't mean the concept is.

Hear me and hear me clearly:

You will not survive this journey without self-care!

Seriously. Divorce can and will consume you if you do not intentionally make sure your body, mind, and spirit are in proper alignment. This starts by prioritizing yourself. Self-care can come in many forms. I categorize those forms as: recreational, spiritual, task-oriented, wellness, and inter/intrapersonal. Let's break these areas down and talk about what it could look like for you.

Recreational: This consists of enjoyable self-care activities such as manipedis, shopping, shooting hoops, hanging with friends/family, etc. Having fun is a necessary component of life. You must have moments where you can find reprieve from the heaviness of your day-to-day. This seems easy, but how often do you trade in girls' night for a nap? Or cancel shooting hoops to go to the grocery store? You must be intentional about scheduling times where you can let loose regularly. Pro-tip: This does not always have to cost money!

Spiritual: How do you care for your spirit-man? Do you set aside time for devotion? Is prayer and meditation a part of your lifestyle? Where is your relationship with God? If you don't know the answers to these questions, or they aren't what you want them to be, you need self-care in this area. In fact, even if you are thriving in your spiritual life, self-care would be maintaining your spiritual lifeline because you will need it each and every day as you journey through healing and recovery.

During times like this, people lose their faith in God, or they use the Word of God to strengthen them. This is not to say you may not question God or have trouble understanding why the divorce occurred, but bring those things to Him and allow Him to provide answers and soothe your soul. Your prayer, devotion, and worship times should be non-negotiable.

Task-Oriented: Self-care can also be practical. During the days when I was most depressed, it was a miracle if I made it out of bed for longer than 30 minutes. I needed task-oriented self-care to make sure my responsibilities got taken care of. Things as simple as eating, taking out the trash, or paying a bill were things that had to be done because they're important. If these don't get accomplished, they can become sources of stress or neglect. Sometimes, having a short to-do list, so you have fewer things to worry about is self-care. What have you been avoiding because of grief, stress, or fatigue? Create a plan to get it done.

Wellness: Say it with me, "I NEED THERAPY!" That's right! You need it. I don't care what you say or think, if you're not in therapy, you are going to struggle more and longer than you have to.

Therapy saved my life and helped me bounce back because I started early on in my process. You need someone who has the tools, time, and tenacity to tend to your "stuff." Your friends, siblings, or parents can't always do it (effectively). However, a counselor can. Make your appointment today.

In addition to therapy, watch your thoughts and what you allow in your mental space. Mind what you're listening to, watching, and even eating as all of these things affect your mental health. You have to check what has real estate in your psyche and choose to evict it if it is not positively impacting your health.

Lastly, **physical wellness** is also an imperative. I maintained a gym regiment for about three months during my separation and divorce. Physical exercise helps with depression, anxiety, and gives you an outlet when you're experiencing high emotions. And if we want to be real.....you'll get your revenge body quicker. I'm just saying!

We will discuss inter/intrapersonal self-care in this season's pause point. In the meantime, let's examine what we've discussed so far.

Season 5 Assignment

Choose **three** self-care activities you will do every day, every week, every month and every year. They should cover all the above categories, if at all possible.

Pause Point

Pause here and take time to watch season 5's video for a more in-depth discussion on self-care. Then use the space below to journal your thoughts.

There are three ways to access the videos:

1. Open your phone's camera app and focus on the QR code. Follow the prompted link.
2. Download a QR code reader app from your apps store and use it to read the code.
3. Go to your web browser and type: www.authenticallywed.com/wscpausepoint.

Season 5 Devotional
Read: Luke 10-38-42

You may find it interesting that I chose the story of Mary and Martha as the devotional for self-care, but when we don't choose to take care of what's most important, we look and sound like Martha. Yes, you have responsibilities and things you need to get done; so did Martha. However, when she should have been taking advantage of having the Son of God in her home and sitting at His feet, she almost missed it by being busy and anxious. Does this sound familiar? Do you make excuses for not spending time in prayer or doing things that would actually strengthen you to accomplish the tasks you have stewardship over? If yes, it's okay. We all do it. However, we can choose to redirect our focus to quiet the thoughts and tasks that attempt to grab our attention and steal our peace.

The greatest self-care you can ever do is prioritizing prayer, meditation, devotion, fasting, and all other spiritual disciplines. Divorce wears on your body, mind, and soul. Only the presence of God can heal and revive those areas. Don't miss Jesus, whom we all so desperately need, for the sake of busyness.

Father, I thank You for a moment of sobriety where I am able to confront the restless state of my heart. Lord, there are so many things calling for my time and attention, and even more on my mind and heart that I don't know what to do. I am overwhelmed and lacking the peace You promised. But today, I choose to sit at Your feet. I willingly lay aside every weight that would try to take me from the path of healing You have set before me (Hebrews 12:1). I choose to steward this vessel You have given me to operate in working order to glorify Your name. I take on Your yoke which is easy and light (Matthew s11:29), and take off the pressure of people-pleasing. Jesus, would You show me what rest looks like for me? Would You show me how to prioritize rest and self-care? I trust You to hold my hand through this journey so that I can come out better and stronger. In Jesus' Name.

Deep Dive

What keeps you from practicing self-care? How can you avoid these obstacles?

How do you feel about you? Often one obstacle with practicing self-care is what we think about ourselves. We make time for what we deem important.

> "Don't expect healed things from broken places."

—Vernique Esther

Thought Space

Use this space to journal any additional thoughts or prayers concerning this season.

Emotional Checkpoint

How do you feel today? Which emotions have you felt most lately? Identify your emotions in the chart and briefly write out your thoughts.

_____
_____
_____
_____
_____
_____

Season 6
My New Normal

I stan for very few things in life, however, I am an unashamed fan of 'The Love Hour' Podcast with Kevin and Melissa Fredericks. In one particular episode on reestablishing trust, Melissa spoke about how in the acting realm, the main character reaches a "point of no return." This is where whatever they're experiencing changes the landscape of the story, thrusting them into a new reality where they will never be the same again.

As the main character in your story, divorce is a defining moment in your life. How defining, however, is up to you. The reality is, you will never, ever be the same again. But why would you want to? Who you were, led you to this place not in a blame-placing way, (but in consequential way). Who you were, made decisions that who you're becoming can't afford to make. Now that you have reached this part of your story, you have two decisions before you: to evolve or be consumed.

Evolution looks like navigating through your feelings, healing (for real), leaning on your support system, being honest with yourself first, then with everyone else, and finding the purpose in the pain. Being consumed looks like making toxic decisions, putting up impenetrable walls, giving up, becoming bitter, putting on a mask of strength, abandoning accountability, and stagnating at this point of pain. Obviously, evolving sounds more desirable, however it's the path that requires the most work and pain upfront. When you become intentional about healing, pain and vulnerability are the down payments.

Right now, your soul and mind are in a state of crisis, similar to that of a person with broken bones. The Healer may have to reset some bones and place you in uncomfortable positions for a season or two. However, in the end, you will be able to say, "It is good for me that I have been afflicted, That I may learn Your statutes" (Psalm 119:71).

So, your new normal will include some brokenness, insecurity, and discomfort...AT FIRST. However, life after divorce can be whatever you make it. God is all about new beginnings; consider this a moment where you say, "The old has passed away and, behold, all things have become new," (2 Corinthians 5:17).

Regardless of what tomorrow and the rest of this journey brings, I promise you, it will not be like this always. Better is coming, and if you look hard enough, it may already be here.

Season 6 Assignment

Write down 10 declarations of who you are and who you are becoming in faith! (ex. I declare that I am healed and whole).

Pause Point

Pause here and take time to watch season 6's video for a more in-depth discussion on your new normal. Then use the space below to journal your thoughts.

There are three ways to access the videos:

1. Open your phone's camera app and focus on the QR code. Follow the prompted link.
2. Download a QR code reader app from your apps store and use it to read the code.
3. Go to your web browser and type: www.authenticallywed.com/wscpausepoint.

_____
_____
_____
_____
_____
_____
_____

Season 6 Devotional
Isaiah 43:19 Isaiah 54:1-6

Welcome to your "new thing." You may not be able to see it quite clearly right now but there is a whole life waiting for you on the other side of this. Actually it's waiting for you NOW. One of the most beautiful signs of healing is hope. In Isaiah 54, the prophet likens Israel to a barren woman who has not given birth.

In this time, it was shameful for a woman of childbearing age to be childless; however, instead of telling her to hide in shame, Isaiah tells her to live BIG. He tells her to enlarge her tent in preparation for the children who will come.

You may feel like the childless woman right now - empty, bare, and ashamed, but I implore you to live BIG! Enlarge your tent and clean house so you can make room for the beautiful life ahead of you. The amazing thing about where you are is, if you feel like you're in a dry desert, Isaiah 43:19 is a reminder that God can spring up a river right where you are. If you feel lost in the wilderness of divorce, He has already created a way out for you.

The only question is: will you be aware? Will you choose to see past where you are and into the hope and future God has for you? Rise and shine, beloved, your light has come (Isaiah 60:1).

Father, I come before You asking You to make me aware of the beauty of where I am. Help me to not shrink back in fear, hurt, and disappointment, but instead to heal and make room for what You have stored up for me. I renounce the thought that my life will end here, and I receive the encouragement and grace to dream and have hope again. I declare that I am not unlovable, but accept the truth that You love me with an everlasting love (Jeremiah 31:3). I declare that I will live and not die and declare the works of the Lord (Psalm 118:17). I declare today that I will not give up because I am confident that I will see the goodness of the Lord while yet in the land of the living (Psalm 27:13), and that my latter days shall be greater than my former (Haggai 2:9). Lord, I choose today to be free from the weight of depression, as I continue to navigate this season, I set my eyes on Jesus, the Author and the Finisher of my Faith (Hebrews 12:2) and I press into my future. In Jesus' Name.

Deep Dive

"And then, after your brief suffering, the God of all loving grace, who has called you to share in his eternal glory in Christ, will personally and powerfully restore you and make you stronger than ever. Yes, he will set you firmly in place and build you up" (1 Peter 5:10 TPT)

What does this Scripture mean to you?

What does living your BEST life look like post-divorce?

What new revelation have you received after going through this devotional? How do you plan to implement things moving forward?

> "Divorce doesn't have to be the end of your life."

-Vernique Esther

Thought Space

Use this space to journal any additional thoughts or prayers concerning this season.

Emotional Checkpoint

How do you feel today? Which emotions have you felt most lately? Identify your emotions in the chart and briefly write out your thoughts.

_____
_____
_____
_____
_____
_____

Author page

Vernique Esther is a metro-Atlanta-based blogger, speaker, entrepreneur, and Licensed Master's Social Worker. She is passionate about Jesus, His Kingdom, people, and creating safe spaces for them to thrive.

Vernique is the founder of Authentically Wed, a blog and online community that focuses on promoting healthy and authentic relationships using Biblical principles. She hopes to use her influence, testimony of divorce, and giftings as a source of freedom and encouragement for all who come in contact with her.

She is a fiercely loyal friend, dedicated conversationalist, and lover of the arts. You can often find her laughing at a gif, sipping warm tea, going on random walks, or simply cuddled up with her laptop, working on her latest idea or event. Though she enjoys her singleness, she is hopeful and excited to, one day, be a loving wife and mother because of the assuredness of the promise of God to her.

"Your latter shall be greater than your former."

To stay connected with, or to contact her:
Website: www.authenticallywed.com
Facebook: Join the "Authentically Wed" group
Instagram: @authenticallywed; @verniqueesther